Other books in this series:
Golf Jokes
Golf Quotations
Teddy Bear Quotations
A Feast of After Dinner Jokes
A Romp of Naughty Jokes

Published in Great Britain in 1991 by
Exley Publications Ltd
16 Chalk Hill, Watford, Herts WD1 4BN, United Kingdom
Reprinted November 1991
Cartoons © Bill Stott 1991. Copyright © Helen Exley 1991.

ISBN 1-85015-259-4

A copy of the CIP data is available from the British Library on request.

Series editor: Helen Exley.
Edited by Samantha Armstrong.
Jokes by Charles Alverson and John Gurney are reproduced by kind
permission of Angus and Robertson Publishers. Jokes from "My Lords,
Ladies and Gentlemen" are reproduced by permission from Piatkus Books.
Cover designed by The Pinpoint Design Company.
Printed by Cambus Litho, East Kilbride.

—A PORTFOLIO OF—

BUSINESS

· J O K E S ·

Cartoons by Bill Stott

5EXLEY

A course for top executives was advertised. "The executive who thinks they have all the answers is the executive who fails. If you are not too sure if you should sign up for this course - you're the person we are looking for."

✳

The company director was an honest man. He admitted that just once, many years before, he had thought he had made a wrong decision.

"But," he added, "it turned out I was mistaken."

✳

The key to being a boss is having a completely clear desk. And a hidden drawer for the rest of the work.

PAM BROWN

✳

Salaries vary according to viewpoint. The factor that determines whether a wage is small or large is whether you are the employer or the employee.

Then there was the sales manager who opened up the sales meeting by announcing:

"Ladies and gentlemen, the purpose of this meeting is to fire you with enthusiasm. If it doesn't work I'm going to fire you – with enthusiasm."

JOHN GURNEY
from *The World's Best Salesman Jokes*

∗

1. The Boss is always right.
2. When the Boss is wrong, refer to Rule 1.

∗

The entire North American sales force of Frisky Dog Food was gathered together for their national sales convention at Miami Beach. In the great auditorium the marketing director was giving a performance that any revivalist would have been proud of. Using the old pattern of call and response, he was really working up the spirits of his sales team.

"Who's got the greatest dog food in North America?"

"We have!"

"And who's got the greatest advertising campaigns?"

"We have!"

"Who's got the most attractive packages?"

"We have!"

"Who's got the biggest distribution?"

"WE HAVE!"

"Okay. So why aren't we selling more of the product?"

One bold voice from the crowd replied:

"Because the damned dogs don't like it."

JOHN GURNEY
from *The World's Best Salesman Jokes*

Business is the art of redefining honesty, fair dealing and acceptable profits.

"WHEN WE TAKE OVER A COMPANY,
WE TAKE THE LOT!"

"Of course I believe in luck. How else can you explain the success of the people you detest?"

JEAN COCTEAU

✳

The junior clerk came out of his boss's office shaking his head.

"What happened?" asked the secretary.

"I'm not sure," said the clerk, "but I think I've been fired."

"What do you mean, you don't know?"

"The boss just looked at me and said: 'Anderson, I don't know how we're going to do without you, but from next week we're going to do our best."

CHARLES ALVERSON
from *The World's Best Business Jokes*

✳

"It is certainly going to be hard to replace you. Especially on the salary we were paying."

✳

"A verbal contract isn't worth the paper it's written on."

SAM GOLDWYN

*

"If you can keep your head when all about you are losing theirs, it is just possible that you haven't grasped the situation."

JEAN KERR
from *Please Don't Eat The Daisies*

"AND THAT WAS PAINTED JUST AFTER WE DISCOVERED HE WAS THE BLACK SHEEP OF THE FAMILY."

A young man shyly crept into the office of the sales manager.

"You don't want to buy any insurance do you?"

"No I don't."

"I thought as much." He turned to go.

"Wait a minute. I've been working with salespeople all my life and I've never seen such a poor approach as yours. You'll never make any sales because you lack confidence. Tell you what I'll do. I'll give you confidence by proving you can make a sale. You can write me up for a life policy."

When the proposal had been completed, the sales manager said:

"Now that you have confidence, you should learn some of the tricks of the trade."

"Thank you very much. You're quite right about the tricks of the trade, of course. The one I just used is for sales managers."

JOHN GURNEY
from *The World's Best Salesman Jokes*

✳

"If at first you don't succeed, try, try, a couple of times more. Then quit: there's no sense in making a fool of yourself."

W. C. FIELDS

THE YUPPIE'S OFFICE DICTIONARY:

Office party.
Source of blackmail for the oncoming year.

Interdepartment football game.
Night of the long knives on a July afternoon.

Over-time.
Time spent doing the work you never quite got round to doing in the day.

Explanation.
Lie.

Convincing explanation.
Inspired lie.

Business lunch.
Lunch.

Liaise.
To leave a message on the answerphone.

"POLLUTION? NONSENSE! I HAVE MY SCIENTISTS WORKING ON PROOF THAT TOO MUCH OZONE IS BAD FOR YOU."

A major business venture.
One that can't be completed by dictating one letter.

Research.
To look up what the last person on the project had found out.

The Board had arranged a secret meeting, to decide how to edge out the Managing Director in order to make way for a younger, sharper brain. Suddenly, the lookout stationed outside opened the office door and whispered loudly, "He's on his way up."

"Oh God," said one man, "we can't be caught like this. Everyone out of the window."

"But we're on the thirteenth floor!"

"Superstitious nonsense. Jump. I'll hold the window open!"

The company's speaking computer was a sensation. So much so that executives kept it so busy answering trivial questions – just to hear it talk – that the work the computer had been bought to do didn't get done.

The head of the computer section got fed up with this and secretly programmed the talking computer with a special answer designed to discourage frivolous and unauthorized use.

The next day, the first person to come into the computer department was the company chairman. Before he could be stopped, the chairman asked the computer: "What is our projected gross profit for this year?"

In response came the programmed answer: "Stop wasting my time with stupid questions and go earn your salary."

CHARLES ALVERSON
from *The World's Best Business Jokes*.

∗

The retired executive was giving some business advice to his son who was just starting up a company.

"In business, ethics are very important. For example, a customer comes in and pays a $100 account in cash. Just as she is leaving you realize that there are two $100 notes stuck together. Do you tell your partner?"

*

The wiliest boss raises controversial points at the meetings called at 4:30 p.m. on Fridays - they get little opposition.

*

No matter how much you do, you'll never do enough.

What you don't do is always more important than what you do do.

"I don't want to achieve immortality through my work. I want to achieve immortality by not dying."

WOODY ALLEN

"AND THAT'S SIR GERALD – NOT OUR MOST POPULAR CHAIRMAN. . . ."

EXCUSES, EXCUSES . . .

"I'm afraid the manager is out at the moment."
"She's standing in the doorway, shaking her
head at me."

"We have decided to widen our researches."
"We need another six months, back off."

"We would be grateful for more information."
"We've lost everything you've sent in so far."

*"We are investigating the matter and will advise you in
due course."*
"We can't find your correspondence."

"We are giving the matter our fullest attention."
"Perhaps if we spin it out long enough you'll forget
all about it."

"When did you say you sent us your claim?"
"I had it. I had it. Where did I put it?"

"Just one moment I have someone on the other line."
"Where's a scrap of paper and a pencil?"

"I am pleased to inform you."
"We've found the damn file at last."

In 1950, legal history was made when an Australian worker won damages from his Melbourne employers because he dislocated his jaw while yawning at work. The courts decided that the damage caused by yawning was an industrial injury. Reason: the man's job was so monotonous he couldn't help yawning.

The Underwriters' Council of Melbourne agreed that in future they would pay full benefit to anyone who was injured through yawning at work.

Bristol Evening Post

If you are absent from work owing to illness or injury on the date on which you join the Plan (or, if this is a non-working day, then on the next preceding working day) you will not be entitled to the death benefit until you return to work.

from a firm's Retirement Benefit Plan

*

"WAIT! THE ACCOUNTANT SAYS
HE WAS ONLY JOKING!"

"Don't trust anybody, not even yourself!"

JAN CREMER

"JUST ONE OF THOSE LITTLE SIGNS THAT TELL THE
KEEN OBSERVER THAT ALL IS NOT WELL."

The incredibly overworked female executive was found by her husband standing glassy-eyed in the hall, apparently caught between making the breakfast, seeing the children off, turning on the washing machine, making out a shopping list and leaving for the office.

She had a puzzled expression on her face. "What on earth's the matter, dear?" asked her husband, well-fed, calm and totally organized.

"Nothing dear, nothing. It's just that for a moment I didn't know whether I was going out or coming in."

PAM BROWN

＊

When I asked my accountant if anything could get me out of the mess I am in now, he thought for a long time . . . "Yes," he said. "Death would help."

ROBERT MORLEY

＊

"Trust everybody, but nobody in particular."

WIM TRIESTHOF

The elegant, exquisitely groomed, utterly assured but aging female executive treated her young and highly qualified personal assistant as an amiable moron.

"Now, my dear, shall I choose from the menu?"

"No, dear, I really don't think that suits you...."

After she had been made to look a fool a dozen times in public, the girl got her revenge...

"Now then, where shall we sit you?"

"Oh Mother darling, anywhere."

*

How to tell a businessman from a businesswoman:

A businessman is aggressive; a businesswoman is pushy. He's good on details; she's fussy. He loses his temper because he's so involved in his job; she's bitchy. He follows through; she doesn't know when to give up. His judgments are her prejudices. He is a man of the world; she's been around. He climbed the ladder of success; she slept her way to the top. He's a stern taskmaster; she's hard to work for.

Today's Woman

The new secretary came into work half an hour late, to be greeted by an angry boss. "You're late!" she roared. "This is not good enough."

"No, I'm not late," replied the secretary, calmly. "I took my lunch break early today – on my way to work."

COMMITTEE RULES

1. Never arrive on time, or you will be stamped a beginner.

2. Don't say anything until the meeting is half over; this stamps you as being wise.

3. Be as vague as possible, this prevents irritating others.

4. When in doubt, suggest that a subcommittee be appointed.

5. Be the first to move for adjournment, this will make you popular - it's what everyone is waiting for.

HARRY CHAPMAN, Think. FD

*

BOREN'S LAWS OF THE BUREAUCRACY

When in doubt, mumble.

When in trouble, delegate.

When in charge, ponder.

JAMES H. BOREN, chairperson of the
International Association of Professional Bureaucrats.

*

There is no one employee so full of ideas and drive as the employee whose boss has just come into the office.

"MORNING FAIRBROTHER – WELCOME TO OSGOOD, OSGOOD AND TREMLETT. I'M TREMLETT AND I'M AN ABSOLUTE SWINE."

"THESE FIGURES ARE VERY DEPRESSING MISS WHITETHIGH –
TAKE TWENTY MINUTES AND HAVE A HEADACHE FOR ME. . . ."

"If you really want a job done, give it to a busy,
important man. He'll have his secretary do it."

CALVIN COOLIDGE

When the typist altered something in a letter that had been dictated, the boss took it as a serious offence.

"I don't pay you to correct my work. Just type it exactly as I say it - don't add anything and don't take anything out."

The next letter that was put in front of the boss to sign went something like this.

"Right then, er, Dear Mr. Smythe, spell that with a 'y' - that's him trying to be posh. In response to your letter of, of, well, you look up the date. We can give you a price of . . . Paul, what kind of price can we give this Smythe guy? OK . . . If he accepts it we better make sure we get payment up front because I really don't trust him. Where's my coffee?

Yours etc etc."

*

An urgent memo was sent by the Managing Director to the senior staff: "We must avoid all unnecessary duplication of communication. I cannot repeat this too many times."

The weary junior was asked by condescending senior partner, "Tell me, which do you think is the real purpose of a holiday? Relaxation? A restoration of energy? The broadening of the mind?"

"Well, actually, I think it's mainly the management's way of reminding each employee that the business can get on perfectly well without them."

*

Work is of two kinds:

1. Altering the position of matter at or near the earth's surface relative to other such matter.

2. Telling other people to do so.

The first is unpleasant and ill paid; the second is pleasant and highly paid.

*

Definition of going on business: *Sightseeing and eating with a dull session in the middle.*

In philosophy a great many ordinary words and phrases are used in a different sense - to create a philosophical vocabulary. The same system is applied in business. 'Honesty', 'integrity' and 'customer's rights' fall into this category.

"GENTLEMEN – WE HAVEN'T TAKEN ANYONE OVER FOR 3.2 WEEKS. ARE WE GOING SOFT?

WHAT BOSSES SAY AND WHAT BOSSES MEAN:

"This is a family firm."
You'll be required to pop out for sandwiches and stay as long as you're needed, with no prior notice.

"If you could glance through this and give me your opinion by tomorrow I would be grateful."
"Cancel everything. You don't need sleep. I want an in-depth analysis on my desk at 9 a.m."

"Please initial and pass on."
"This way you all share the blame if I've made a mistake."

"Well then, how do you see it?"
"Go on, make a complete fool of yourself."

"See me."
"Start praying."

"Thank you for bringing this error to our attention."
"Blast you."

"I like employees to give me their frank opinion."
"Watch it."

"Let's get together on this."
"I'm assuming you're as confused as I am."

"NOBODY CAN SAY SHE'S HAD IT
EASY ON HER WAY TO THE TOP. . . ."

Seeking his first job, a young man wrote this question on his application form: "Are the salary increases here automatic or do you have to work to earn them?"

✳

"Once you have started doing nothing at all, you have to persevere."

JOHAN ANTHIERENS

"THE EMPLOYEES'S FREE SAMPLE SCHEME IS BEING ABUSED...."

In the 1940s when Mark Woods was president of the American Broadcasting Company an employee managed to slip by his secretary into his office.

"I just had to see you, Mr. Woods," he said in desperation. "I've asked my supervisor for a raise and he said that I couldn't have one. But I really ought to get more money."

"Why?" demanded Woods.

"Well, there are three companies that want me."

"What three companies?"

"The electricity company, the gas company and the phone company," said the employee.

He got the raise - in recognition of his initiative and humorous explanation!

∗

Because of my short-sightedness I almost worked myself to death – I couldn't tell whether the boss was watching me or not so I had to work all the time . . . until I got my new glasses!

∗

To err is human but to really foul things up requires a computer.

*"THERE'S SOMETHING BOTHERING YOU,
ISN'T THERE, MISS BRAITHWAITE?"*

Working with a computer would send you mad if you didn't give it a name and a personality. As soon as you've scolded it once or twice, and given it a promotion when it comes up with the right answer - then you've got the problem licked.

PAM BROWN

*

CORCORAN'S LAW OF PACKRATTERY
All files, papers, memos, etc that you save will never be needed until such time as they are disposed of when they will become essential and indispensable.

JOHN CORCORAN, writer and TV personality.

*

A study on the productivity of workers took four years to complete. It found that the employee who whistles and sings at work never produces as much as the person who moans and groans continuously. It is the employee who complains the loudest and most often about the job, the company and the boss who has the highest output.

When you hear, "We're having a little trouble with the computer." It means, "We've lost everything...."

"LOOK – I'M SORRY – PLEASE DON'T GO BLANK –
I DIDN'T MEAN TO SAY YOU WERE STUPID. . . ."

DEFINITIONS

Definition of a Secretary: *The only person who knows how, why, when and if.*

Definition of a Senior Executive: *Anyone with an office on the carpeted corridor.*

Definition of a Statistician: *One who knows which numbers to use in any eventuality.*

Definition of a Colleague: *The person to whom one passes the buck.*

Definition of a Conference: *Time off from the hurly burly of hard graft and actual thought.*

Definition of a Filing cabinet: *A useful container where things can be lost alphabetically.*

Definition of an Informed source: *Him.*

Definition of a Salesman: *A fellow with a smile on his face, a shine on his shoes, and a lousy territory.*

The accounts clerk was chasing a customer for payment and had sent several "final reminders" but to no avail. Eventually, a phone call was necessary. When the call was put through to the right department, the frustrated clerk was told, "The Director whose signature is needed is laid up with a sprained ankle."

"So?" exclaimed the fuming clerk. "Do they sign them with their feet?"

*

A rep found himself stranded by torrential rain, totally unable to continue his set round of calls. He wired head office, "Trapped by floods. Send instructions."

The reply came at once, "Annual leave granted, commencing today."

*

"If you don't want to work, you have to work to earn enough money so that you won't have to work."

OGDEN NASH

It is said that, when George Washington's secretary was late and blamed it on his watch, the first president of the US replied, "Then you must find another watch, or I another secretary."

✳

"AND HERE'S A QUESTIONNAIRE FROM PERSONNEL ABOUT WHETHER YOU PREFER A MALE OR FEMALE BOSS. I'LL TELL YOU WHICH BOXES TO TICK."

The industrial psychologist was testing all employees of a large firm. To impress the unions, the boss insisted he should be included. His answers were commonplace until the question,

"How do you react to criticism?"

"N/A."

*

When he was the US secretary of state, Henry Kissinger is said to have looked at his calendar and told one of his aides,

"There cannot be a crisis next week. My schedule is already full."

*

Being boss is when any mistake you make is acceptable, being seen as a bold experiment.

*

A young man who had recently inherited a small fortune had heard about the advances in modern transplant surgery, and decided he would benefit from a new brain. He went to see a specialist and asked him what he could offer.

"Well," said the specialist, "that depends on what you can afford. At the moment we have several brains in stock: that of a bank-clerk for £5,000, a University professor for £10,000 or a High Court judge for £20,000."

"I am a wealthy man," said the young man. "Tell me, what is your absolute best and most expensive one at the moment?"

"You are in luck," said the specialist, "we happen to have a stockbroker's, a very special offer at £50,000."

"I don't understand," said the young man, "why is a stockbroker's brain so much more expensive than any of the others?"

"Simple, it's hardly ever used," said the specialist.

THE LATE LORD BRABAZON OF TARA
from *My Lords, Ladies & Gentlemen.*

"SOMETHING TELLS ME THERE ARE GOING TO BE SOME CHANGES AROUND HERE. . . ."

The long term employee was called into the boss's office last thing on Friday.

"The important thing about your job is that it requires a person of great experience, quick-thinking, resourcefulness and determination. And that's why I called you in, I think you should retire. . . ."

✳

The shop stewards had swung the perfect deal. The chief shop steward addressed the members.

"Alright, everyone," he said, "we've won. Wages up by 50%, two months paid holiday, cordon bleu chef in the canteen - and you only have to work one day in a week."

An indignant voice called from the back. "Does that mean every Friday?"

A factory advertised for workers. The response revealed just how bad the unemployment situation was in the area. Three of those who applied answered the question "Salary expected", "yes".

WHEEL CLAMP AT YOUR PERIL

In a row of small shops one shopkeeper was becoming unnerved by the huge hard-sell signs going up in his rivals' windows:

PRICES CUT TO THE BONE

NOWHERE CHEAPER

SERVICE. SMILES. SATISFACTION.

QUALITY YOU CAN AFFORD

He sat down and thought. And put up just one sign across his doorway, in bold but dignified print:

MAIN ENTRANCE

PAM BROWN

✳

The circus advance person asked the cost of taking a full page advertisement in the local paper. The price seemed pretty steep.

"What about a half page?" The same. "A quarter?" The same. "What are you playing at? There's no sense in that!"

"Plenty of sense. We're the only local paper, you need the space. And I've a bill due for exactly that amount, day after you open."

The lower Manhattan branch of Brook Brothers was robbed. The thieves escaped with clothes valued at $200,000. One clerk complained:

"If they had come during our sale two weeks ago, we could have saved 20 per cent."

from *The Book of Business Anecdotes*

"LIKES TO KEEP IN TOUCH WITH HIS ROOTS – COMES TO WORK IN A DIFFERENT STOLEN CAR EVERY DAY."

The office junior was looking for a safe place to leave the secretary's parting gift.

"Put it in my filing cabinet", advised the boss, "nothing is ever found in there".

"HE CAN BE A BIT SNAPPY IN THE MORNINGS. . . ."

Aaron, who couldn't sleep at night, was tossing and turning, and finally his wife said, "Aaron, what is it, I can't bear it any longer, something must be worrying you, you can tell me what it is." So eventually, in the middle of the night, he says, "Well, I've been trying to keep it from you Miriam, but now I'll tell you: The terrible thing is, that I owe my friend Moishe money. I owe him £500, I can't pay it, I don't know where I can get the money from and I can't sleep at nights for worrying about it. What can I do?"

His wife thinks for a few minutes and says, "Aaron, I can't bear to have you worrying so much and unable to sleep at night. I will tell you what to do. You will tell your friend Moishe that you can't pay him the money. And then you can let *him* worry."

KATHARINE WHITEHORN
from *My Lords, Ladies & Gentlemen*.

✳

Trying to conceal from my boss the fact that I was typing out a psychology report for my brother, who is an undergraduate, I slipped it under a stack of mail. A few minutes later, forgetting about the report, I took the mail into my boss. At the end of the day I realized what I had done, and asked if he had seen it. He had. So had the vice-chairman, and the executives at head office. Everybody had signed it, but not one of them knew what to do with it – or what it had to do with them.

KATHLEEN FARLOW

"THAT'S YOUR COMPANY CAR. . . ."

"WELL, IT'S NOT A GOOD SIGN, THAT'S FOR SURE."

The executive in conference with an important client spoke into the intercom.

"Miss Jones. Get me my broker."

Miss Jones, sick and tired of being exhibited as an efficient robot purred her reply.

"Certainly, Mr. Baggins. Stock or pawn?"

✳

"HAVEN'T YOU HEARD, AFTER THE BOARDROOM RE-SHUFFLE, WE LOST OUR COMPANY CARS BUT KEPT OUR DRIVERS. . . ."

"I thought you might be interested. The company's looking for a treasurer."

"But surely they filled that vacancy?"

"Oh yes, last month. That's the one they're looking for."

✳

When clearing out her filing cabinets, Samuel Goldwyn's secretary wanted to destroy some of the old files to make room for the more recent ones.

"Go ahead," the movie mogul replied, "but make sure you keep copies."

"THE CHAIRMAN DOES THAT FROM TIME TO TIME TO KEEP US ON OUR TOES...."

The one thing that disturbed the boss was coming into the office and finding all of the employees he paid to work just sitting around gossiping and not working, so he called together his entire staff.

"Now, see here," he told them, "I'm a fair sort of chap, and I know there must be a better way to organize things so that when I arrive in the morning I don't find you just wasting time. So I'm putting up a suggestion box, and I hope that I'll find the answer in it."

At the end of the day when everybody had gone home, he opened up the suggestion box and to his surprise found only a single slip of paper in it with the following typed on it: "Stop wearing rubber-soled shoes."

CHARLES ALVERSON
from *The World's Best Business Jokes*

✳

Those proud of keeping an orderly desk never know the thrill of finding something they thought they had irretrievably lost.

"When you don't know what to do, walk fast and look worried."

BOB DUCKLES

*

"THE MANAGER'S ON HIS WAY. . . ."